Addendum to a Miracle

Addendum to a Miracle

Mike White

WAYWISER

First published in 2017 by

THE WAYWISER PRESS

Christmas Cottage, Church Enstone, Chipping Norton, Oxfordshire, OX7 4NN, UK
P.O. Box 6205, Baltimore, MD 21206, USA
https://waywiser-press.com

Editor-in-Chief
Philip Hoy

Senior American Editor
Joseph Harrison

Associate Editors
Eric McHenry | Dora Malech | V. Penelope Pelizzon | Clive Watkins
Greg Williamson | Matthew Yorke

Copyright © Mike White, 2017

The right of Mike White to be identified as the author of this work
has been asserted by him in accordance with the
Copyright, Designs and Patents Act of 1988.

All rights reserved. No part of this publication may be reproduced, stored in
a retrieval system, or transmitted in any form or by any means, electronic,
mechanical, photocopying, recording, or otherwise, without the prior permission
of both the copyright owner and the above publisher of this book.

9 7 5 3 1 2 4 6 8

A CIP catalogue record for this book is available from the British Library

ISBN 978-1-904130-89-5

MIX
Paper from responsible sources
FSC® C013056

Printed and bound by
T. J. International Ltd., Padstow, Cornwall, PL28 8RW

This book is dedicated to the memory of Bill and Audrey Fagg

Acknowledgments

Grateful acknowledgment to the editors of the following magazines in which these poems first appeared, sometimes in earlier versions:

Birmingham Poetry Review: "Will" and "Snow Globe"
Cider Press Review: "Reading Chekhov at the Laundromat"
Cimarron Review: "Forest"
Connecticut Review: "Age of Miracles"
Denver Quarterly: "Today's Decapitation" and "Elegy"
Ecotone: "Early Morning at the Petting Zoo"
The Fiddlehead: "God" and "Sunday School"
FIELD: "Pigeon," "Break," "Ark," and "Angel"
The Green Hills Literary Lantern: "Deli, Montreal"
Green Mountains Review Online: "Addendum to a Miracle" and "Piano"
The Greensboro Review: "Alley in Winter"
Interim: "The Day Comes" and "Titanic"
Literature and Belief: "The Reading Lamp," "Imprint," "Rain Clods," and "Easter"
The Malahat Review: "Nothing"
New Letters: "Fable"
The Normal School: "Frequency"
Ploughshares: "Reunion"
Poet Lore: "House after a Tornado," "Vigil," "After the Silent Era," and "The Elephants"
Poetry East: "Love" and "Family Album"
Poetry International: "Holocaust"
Rattle: "Fathers," "Arms," "So, If Everyone Else Jumped Off a Bridge," and "Watch"
Spillway: "One Small Step" and "Nature"
Sycamore Review: "Go Ahead"
Tar River Poetry: "Dying"
The Threepenny Review: "Things Pitched"
West Branch: "A Thing of Beauty," "Contrail," and "Substitute"
Witness: "Migration"
The Yale Review: "Nativity"

Acknowledgments

The author also gratefully acknowledges the following online publications for reprinting poems in this book that first appeared elsewhere: *Poetry Daily*, *Verse Daily*.

* * *

Thank you to the poets and readers and editors who have provided feedback on these poems, especially Joseph Harrison, Philip Hoy, Jacqueline Osherow, Donald Revell, and Gjertrud Schnackenberg.

Thanks must also go to my entire family, and to my mother and grandmother in particular for reading to me, many moons ago.

And, of course, thank you to Chrisa and Kaemon — for every moment.

Contents

Foreword by Gjertrud Schnackenberg   11

Alley in Winter   15

ONE

Nativity	19
The Day Comes	20
Deli, Montreal	21
Addendum to a Miracle	23
A Thing of Beauty	24
Go Ahead	25
Reunion	26
Fathers	27
Arms	28
Piano	29
One Small Step	30
Leavings	31
Mobile	34
Contrail	36
Pigeon	37
The Reading Lamp	38
Age of Miracles	39

TWO

Imprint	43
Story	44
Fable	45
So, If Everyone Else Jumped Off a Bridge	46
Break	48
God	49
Ark	50
Will	51
Snow Globe	52
Rain Clods	53
House after a Tornado	54

Contents

Snowman	55
Watch	56
Early Morning at the Petting Zoo	57
Migration	58
"Brandon's Nuts Hang Down to the Water"	59

THREE

Vigil	67
Love	68
Nursing Home	69
Reading Chekhov at the Laundromat	70
Sunday School	71
Holocaust	72
Dying	74
Family Album	75
Titanic	76
Forest	77
Nature	78
Easter	79
Things Pitched	80
Substitute	81
Nothing	82
After the Silent Era	83
Today's Decapitation	84
Elegy	85
Frequency	86
The Elephants	87
Angel	88

A NOTE ABOUT THE AUTHOR	91
A NOTE ABOUT THE ANTHONY HECHT POETRY PRIZE	93

Foreword by Gjertrud Schnackenberg

Mike White's short poems, sometimes no more than a single sentence, repeatedly take on, for all their brevity — like an ant carrying a leaf — a large and looming question: *how could the world possibly be as it is?* After choosing his manuscript, and learning his name, I looked him up on the Internet, and found his description of his love for the poetry of Issa; immediately I saw the spiritual connection. Although Mike White does not write haiku, and he is not a nature poet, and his gods, present or absent, are not Issa's, and although his voice is a thoroughly 21st century, Western voice, the lines of his spiritual descent from Issa shine clearly. White's poems, like Issa's, are egoless, unknowing, and profoundly surprised. Like Issa's works of "one-breath" world-making, his poems come into existence as bubbles, momentary worlds blown into being by the breath of comedy.

For example, the poet's recurring, poem-by-poem premonition that the creation may be, among other things, a comedy of errors, gains traction in "Rain Clods," a poem in which we behold the poet, framed within a frame, typing out the very poem we are reading. He makes a typo right at the start, as he types the title. Typos are meaningless non-events, a dime a million, too trivial even to bother to overlook. But in the fraction-second in which he sees his mistake, seeing that the innately humorous word "clod" embodies the mistake it inadvertently describes, which perhaps innocently reflects its self-description back upon the erring typist-poet — in that fraction of a second, the poet's mind lies open, surprised, to a great pouring-in of sympathetic correspondences. With a missed stroke, the "u" is left out, and the word's molecular structure is rearranged: cloud turns into clod, and "clod" rings a tiny rhyme-bell with the creator's name, and, as if in response, "the sky opens/ as never before." The heavens, usually caught up with declaring the glory of God, shift their energies over to the feat of being funny. Among the clods of rain, the God-particle glints.

Comedy in this poetry is unclassifiable (in much the same way that poetry itself is indefinable), its gradations unnotated and unnumbered, like the range of vibrations between C# and D, D# and E. The comedy in *Addendum to a Miracle* is not of the widespread, world-spread cynical, unforgiving ilk, not caustic or corroding; it isn't tethered to the vein-drip of irony, or packed in dry-ice wit like a heart that has been cut out of its chest. His humor is a healing, not a wounding, perception, suffusing its human portraits with intimations, intuitions, and intonations. Long ago I discovered Aristotle's sentence that "Tragedy and comedy come from the same letters;" and I have pictured ever since the alphabet, in light of that insight, as letters forever engaged — either way, tragedy or comedy — in spelling out the word "human." In Mike White's poems, humanity is a one-by-one, wondrous eventuation, and he presents human beings front and center, in deft portraits which are funny or throbbingly painful or both: the dad with his family in tow, making his getaway from church, his loosened tie flapping out the open car window; the substitute teacher who, with a profane outburst, turns her "scalding eyes" on her pupil-tormentors; the homeless man who could be reaching into his tattered parka for a knife, but who instead turns out to be offering an apple core, in an incident whose absurdity floats beyond laughter; the redoubtable, elderly Goldfinger.

White loves speed, acceleration, momentum — and he finesses their necessary counterpart, reversal. He is a speed-skater on the white page, and the brevity of his poems is a consequence of his speed (speed is time going fast, and, as time speeds up, it reduces space). By the time we have begun to read one of these poems, the poem is nearly over, hurtling toward its end, and what space is left is shrinking to a vanishing point. The speed-brevity (and clarity) of these poems makes the poems easy to read, but they must be hell to write, and it doesn't help that, contrary to contemporary theories that poetry is nothing but language, nothing but a barrage of words, this poet works as if he believes poetry's words are suspended among forces, strong and weak, which exist around and beyond them. I sense the labor of their making, and I groan to think of what these poems have cost their author in hours, days, weeks, months, years. I think a portrait of the immensity of the labor required heaves into view in the poem "Piano," where a piano is being hoisted, inch by inch, up a stairway, with gargantuan effort, one step at a time, by non-professional movers. In the absence of proper equipment, they have nothing but sheer human will and strength for the all-focusing, all-else-forgetting purpose of pulling the massive instrument up and out of the clutches of gravity (with muttered "mother-of-gods"), as the stairwell abyss, lying open below them, deepens with every successful hoist. This labor is undertaken solely for the sake of music-making, with no miracles of help on offer, and, as such, it pictures a situation surely familiar to most writers. And yet this portrait of human labor overflows with human comedy — and hints, too, at divine comedy — in describing the "slow inglorious agony/ of ascension."

Miracles, defined in the dictionary as the "extraordinary deeds of God," are of course reserved for the deity. One of God's extraordinary deeds, for example, is recorded in the book of Job: *He hangeth the earth upon nothing*. This is the God of one Mr. Goldfinger, whose radiantly comic portrait takes up all the space of White's masterpiece poem, "Holocaust." Through the eyes of a child, playing among other children in a swimming pool, we see the old man, heavily ensconced in a lounge chair, poolside. To the children, he is a conglomeration of broken English, unwieldy physics, empty threats, and joy in life, with his suntan oil, and his mesmerizingly outsized ring, flashing in the sunlight. He points his hugely beringed finger at the cannonballing boys, issuing brusque orders and warnings: "*No splashes, you kids, or maybe/ you want I come in*." The children easily perceive the ill-concealed tenderness of this august, kingly personage; they can't take their eyes off of him. The poem is wonderful fun as it flies headlong to its end, but it is forced into an emergency pivot before a sudden dark wall, as high and deep as the cosmos. I think of Alexander Pope's couplet from his *Essay on Man*:

> *Atoms and systems into ruin hurl'd;*
> *And now a bubble burst; and now a world.*

In this poem, and in others, I seem to see the poet stumble over a large bolt of fabric, which he picks up wonderingly — tragedy its eternal warp, comedy its glinting weft — and then holds up in front of himself, with his arms outstretched overhead, like a magician's curtain. I fall for the apparent distraction, motionless, watching the curtain, presuming that he is hiding his preparations for his next spectacle. It takes me more than a moment to realize that the magician has departed the stage. And the fabric still is hanging in midair.

Alley in Winter

    May the body
    of work be

    beautiful
    as the fire

    escape is
    beautiful

    dazzled in ice
    after the fire

One

Nativity

I am the one
who took the photo,

the one
who on a frigid moonless night
was summoned, instructed
to rise from a warm bed,

to arrange the baffled animals,
to adjust, over and over,
for light.

The Day Comes

The fly
desists,

stands
and looks
out the window,

a housefly.

Deli, Montreal

It is my first job.
I am fifteen
and lousy at everything.
The old man holds my wrist.
I try to slice the meat thin, thin.
I try hard not to break plates.

In my ear he tells me
again and again
about that time
before your father even was born.

I don't want to listen.
I want to quit this place that stinks
of things hanging from hooks.
My life, I wonder, my real life,
will it ever begin?

But he leans in close
and this time it's about
soldiers marching, marching

like this, like this, you understand

and the uncle or the nephew
gone for bread
and never heard from again

and the women
good women
lined up against a wall

thin boy thin,

Deli, Montreal

like something,
he says to me,
something you have never seen …

*you in this lucky country,
and how can you know what I mean,
you in this big lucky country?*

Addendum to a Miracle

And then, after
asking for silence, and
for silence please, and
for silence way in the back please,

he made of the many fishes
(churning silver
in the brimful baskets)

                    just one
irrefutable fish, size
of a single loaf of bread,

and the mouths of the multitude
watered, and
the gills of the dying fish
fanned the poison air.

A Thing of Beauty

I want my goldfish
back. By goldfish
I mean childhood
when orange was all
the rage. Davy ate his
alive and changed
schools after setting
fire to enough things.
The way through
the dark what is it?
With terrible secret words
I cheered Davy on
and he shone.

Go Ahead

Go ahead and
put Auschwitz
on the spelling test

it is late spring
you are hated

what happens
happens

Reunion

And shall we describe the beautiful bike?
It was a beautiful color the beautiful bike.
What ever happened to the beautiful bike?
The beautiful bike rode off into the beautiful sunset.
Not by itself, surely. Who was pedaling the beautiful bike?
You, you were the one pedaling the beautiful bike
last seen disappearing into the beautiful sunset.

Now I remember the beautiful bike.
Now I can see myself
pedaling like mad the beautiful bike …

Is it okay to cry?
It is always okay to cry.

It is *so* good to see you again.
It is so good to see *you* again.

Fathers

This one saws the board.
This one sees the board
but does not saw it, or not
as *his* father sawed it.
This one saws
his kids in half
but does not see it.
This one is bored.
This one still sees what he saws,
his second wife says.
This one saws to have something
real to seize.
This one for the scent of pine.
This one for the sound.
This one sees saws
as everything around him
comes slowly crashing down.

Arms

Angels do not exist.
Bombs exist.

At someone's say-so,
they fall from the clouds,
they carry you off,

you, who to them
weigh nothing.

Piano

To the movers
paid in pizza

and sweating
in a darkening stairwell,

no moonlight sonata,
but a moon, of a kind, imposing

its shadowy grandeur and girth,
its unrelenting pull upon the earth

felt along make-do ropes, straps,
lines that quiver and work

deep into the flesh, deeper
groans, mother-of-gods, and another

concerted heave to surmount
a single step, this

slow inglorious agony
of ascension.

One Small Step

On his last journey, Bashō
discovers the moon
shining full in his wooden bowl,

and having grown
light as a thought, steps
out and into

               white space

Leavings

out of the endless
transport train and into
the morning sky

eyes
for scarcely anything
but the Museum itself

an old mosaic,
the cement binding
the various little stones

empty bowls, waiting
for the next payday,
speaking of it

a longing, in it lies
a well
which never grows dry

brighter light flared up,
only to vanish again
in the spectral darkness

harder that I was numbered
among the nameless, that I
was one of the millions

Leavings

in my hand
a suitcase full
of clothes and underwear

the little pellets
flying between our ranks,
ripping up the wet ground

a maggot in a rotting body,
dazzled
by the sudden light

an apparition
in a black caftan
and black hair locks

the beat
of its innermost heart,
the other

and everywhere,
the eternal mushroom
of humanity

to swing
back again and
again to the old madness

Leavings

a stone
had been set
rolling

a few points
and repeat them
over and over

the fox is always
a fox, the goose
a goose

what intolerable pranks
this 'Hitler'
played

my eyes had turned
into glowing coals,
it had grown dark around me

to see the road
in small
partial sketches

a thousand ways,
every one of which
ends in a weapon

– selected passages from *Mein Kampf*, Volume I (1925)

Mobile

A racist,
she loves birds,

assigns them
bright sweet names

from a chair
by the window,

forgets …

after lunch
the staff knows

to fetch her
on the double

a thick wad
of napkins

out of which
with trembling hands

she fashions
birds, birds

the orderly
hangs for her,

a small darkish
figure who,

as shadows
fall and night grows

Mobile

around the chair
by the window,

sweeps up.

Contrail

Real as insurance
the sky
its dome of blue.

A cloud obscures
the incision,

a little sleep
we come round to.

Pigeon

I am in the station,
only I am
not taking the train.

A rock, a dove,
below, above,

I am God's
good eye,

waiting out the rain.

The Reading Lamp

allows
the living

room
to be

other
wise
dark

Age of Miracles

Upon a darkening hill
the telescopes turn as one.

They say the stars will fall
by and by, on and on.

Two

Imprint

Snow keeps falling
on fallen snow,
unmaking the wings
of a child I know.

Story

Of the finger caught
beneath the skate blade
we must never speak.

It was not my fault.
It was not my finger.

It was never found.
It never happened.
It was lying

in the goal mouth.

Fable

A whale's heart
minus the whale
washed up on the beach.

The war was on.

The newspaper reported on it
below an advert for *Real
Meat in a Can!*

The thinking was
it might explode.

The children had to be
told and told
not to touch it.

And given its size
and dazzling arrangement of living parts,
not to enter.

So, If Everyone Else Jumped Off a Bridge

I'd never
get over the loneliness.
I'd be surprised as all hell.
I'd say it like a sutra: *everyone*.
I'd rave, I'd mourn, I'd sulk, I'd run out of food
and have to go shopping.
I'd bring along a credit card and a driver's license.
I'd roll through stop signs, nervously.
I'd maneuver my shopping cart through the cavernous aisles,
reading the advertised specials, as if
I was taking part in a zombie movie, becoming
by turns the victim, the zombie, the actor.
I'd wonder at the sheer number of mirrors in the world.
I'd go to bed early, thinking, I'm going to wake up and …
I'd be afraid to go out at night, like a refugee, like a woman.
I'd stop showering because someone
might be on the other side of the curtain with a knife
now that there was no one to protect me, now that there was no
    one.
I'd stop showering just because I could.
I'd start thinking that maybe this all meant I was immortal
which I had long suspected was the case
and then I'd reason that just because everyone else
had jumped off a bridge it didn't follow that I was going to live
    forever.
I'd want to die much of the time.
I'd stop writing poems, nothing more
than a mild shock, like opening the fridge in the middle of the
    night
to find the power had gone out.
I'd read the same shit differently, and by candlelight eventually.
I'd translate the faces in the photo album into Braille.
I'd scan the dawn sky for airplanes, the hedges for lost pets.
I'd cry for joy hearing a sparrow, a cricket, whatever.
I'd know the month and the day of the week so help me God.
I'd drive to bridges and then to *the* bridge,

So, If Everyone Else Jumped Off a Bridge

iron railings in a rolling fog.
I'd gaze down and into
the onrushing water, into my
own improbable shadow.

Break

Off the interstate
a girl in the traditional
if not My Little Pony sense
of the term who works
I'm guessing three nights a week
at McDonald's can be seen
speed-limping in full uniform
across eight lanes of stop and go
traffic to meet her boyfriend (not
a boy) in the blotchy shadows
behind the Wendy's parking lot.

There they are, half-hidden, half-,
when he bends to light
her cigarette from his cupped hands,
their cap brims touching
in the sudden orange aura.

I think *crush*
and in the same breath,
crèche.

Here is someplace that is
never not light,
and the stars, as a consequence,
do not shine, do not work.

God

we say,
meaning something

hidden, like the self-
talker who lurches

boozily into my path
one night and then reaches

into the greasy hollows
of his over-large parka
searching for what

must be a knife – or
a green apple.

In no world
but ours

would I be
offered the core.

Ark

The small shy animals
that go on

breeding and dying
in the condemned house

left more open than not
to seed drift and starlight

God be praised

still have no one
to answer to

Will

What could go wrong at a circus?
Dad will have trouble parking.
The horses will gallop in a perfect circle.
The holding of hands, or getting lost,
no third alternative.
The souvenirs will be expensive, will be out

of the question. And then
the elephant who mulled over what if
in Laramie and Evanston and Pocatello
will decide tonight to put his foot down,
and you won't be able to look
away when it happens.

Snow Globe

Nothing that rough god
could do about the snow

but move it from place
to place.

We nursed our coughs inside
the country church
and watched the weather.

Spring always seeming
right around the corner,

if only
there were a corner.

Rain Clods

An innocent slip
at the typewriter,

and God ...

God not being one
to waste a perfectly
good word,

the sky opens
as never before.

House after a Tornado

Here is moonlight
scattered piecemeal across
a cardboard-thin kitchen wall.

And somewhere, far into the night,
the dull shine of dime-sized plates
and the long level gaze of a doll.

Snowman

Like all men
he was composed
of three layered parts.

An ill-fitting hat.
Stones for eyes.

Very silent.
Very cold.

We stood well back
to admire him.

One fine sunny day …

For a while
he sent money.

Watch

dog roped to a tree,
perfecting a circle
in the leaves,
in the snow,
in the grass.

Early Morning at the Petting Zoo

Maintenance is out
smoking in brown coveralls,
dragging shovels.

In the shadow
of the ferris wheel,
bright hints of deer.

Migration

They would say no
forget the bird
there is no bird
there

and all winter long
you'd not stop
saying

bird bird bird

insisting

in your big mysterious bed
upon some
bright live thing

come all this way

"Brandon's Nuts Hang Down to the Water"

In the Reno bus station,
in the stall furthest
from the yogic exertions
of a man washing his feet
in the sink,
I give myself over
to thinking about Brandon,

to wondering who needed him
enough to leave this tribute
carved as much as written
in dark red ink
above the toilet paper dispenser.

I read into things.

Like the notice scotch-taped
to the ticket window
warning of pickpockets,
which has me half-hiding here,
examining for comparison's sake
my own considerably
less elastic scrotum.

Or that grainy photo
(the only one that could be found?)
of the little girl
with the goofy gap-toothed smile,

last seen …
the year before my son was born.

Shit.

Shit.

"Brandon's Nuts Hang Down to the Water"

Where does it go?

It just disappears, forever,
swirled into a cosmic vortex and
sucked down a gleaming bowl, a loss
which every put-upon toddler knows
to be a basic violation of personhood.

How very different in the days
of the outhouse: a *house*,
say what you will, in its own right,
consisting of a wagonload
of warped and mismatched boards,
a splintery seat and shallow pit;

a place to sit and think and watch
the spiders spin their eloquent webs,
and listen at a settled distance
to the human weather inside.

No spiders here;
just a pencil-drawn swastika
that, if I squint, almost looks the part.
It's small, hardly there, as if
offered in the spirit
of a tentative suggestion.

And the others, who've left
no trace of themselves …

The man with pink lipstick
on his wilted penis
and the one
who sweats through his shirt
waiting for a shoe

"Brandon's Nuts Hang Down to the Water"

to push the promised bag of powder
from the adjoining stall.

And the ones on their knees,
fishing with a finger
for a quarter, a key, a ring,
a missing tooth ...

Brandon, always you find us
out, with pants down
around our ankles, washed up
on some strange shore, searching

like Crusoe
for a coin-operated box
that will dispense
four varieties of condoms, only

tonight there's a strip of duct tape
across the money slot, and a sign

that reads No More Sorry.

By the waters of Babylon,
the Israelites, exiles, captives
in a hostile land,
hung their harps from willows
and refused to play.

I can all but see
those abandoned harps now, still
bending the branches
above the darkened river, maybe
swaying slightly in the breeze,
and yielding, in spite of everything,
a soft soulful music.

"Brandon's Nuts Hang Down to the Water"

In spite of everything, Brandon,
you are here, in the bowels
of the human town,

confessor and custodian
of our shared
privacies, our comings
and goings, you

more-than hear, you overhear
the chronic sigh, the stifled sob,
the air guitar of prayer,

because you are, Brandon, and have always been,
a talisman to bring the rain
and swell the corn,

a clay vessel to fill
with bear's blood, and spill with chanted rites
upon the belly of a newlywed.

As a rule, nothing grows in Reno –
but in the rich permissive shadows
of your hanging garden,
this toilet water becomes
the reflective surface
of a koi pond
into which a moon rises
and a poet from his hut
rises to write it down.

Now I can't help seeing you
in the balled fists of a scared child
unclenching in sleep,

"Brandon's Nuts Hang Down to the Water"

and now
in the extravagant breasts
of an old woman
laughing up and down in the mirror.

There's no keeping your story
straight, Brandon,

you split the seams,

male and female both, singing
the body eccentric,

singing

no more sorry,
no more sorry.

Meanwhile the man at the sink is finished.
I can see his clean bare feet.
There is no other place for him.
He walks around in his clean bare feet,
on tiptoe, making as little noise as an angel,
as little noise as can be.

Three

Vigil

There it was
the cave
full of my smell

and dragged-in
things.

Late winter
and still

I stood watching
in the snow
for whatever

should emerge.

And just to kill
the time I wrote

love notes

and placed them
there
at the stony mouth

to blossom
or melt.

Love

You mean the world to me, meaning
the only way to see you
is from outer space.
As you know
I have little aptitude
for space travel.
Like the monkey
they launched into orbit
I tend to push buttons at random
and eat too much people food.
Where am I going with this thing? I know
the dark is all around us, love.
I'm out here waving to you, only to you,
round and green and blue.

Nursing Home

The stars, too, are gassy
and immoveable.

Hard inscrutable suns
blazing for another world,

they leak light,
                       and are

seen to
as time allows,

night after night after night.

Reading Chekhov at the Laundromat

A civil servant with a lump in his throat
brushes up against a married woman's arm
under the trestles of a bridge;
a complicated Russian sky;
a sentry on the bridge running
his hand through his hair.
I watch over my somersaulting socks,
their hypnotic fabric-softened swirl.
The winter months pass imperceptibly.
The smell of stale pipe tobacco
lingers in the closed rooms.
An old woman yawns
and puts the samovar on to boil.
I drop another quarter into the dryer,
stare absently as a young woman
holding a screaming child under one arm
pleads with the change machine
to accept her crumpled dollar.
Some loose talk is made
of going to St. Petersburg,
but nothing comes of it.
A baby is born into the margin.
Then one day spring arrives.
A thrush is heard. Or maybe
it was the tinkle of a piano
being played in another room
that caused dark hairs to rise invisibly
upon a braceleted arm:
Why, oh, why have you come?
The evening breeze is thick with lilac scent.
The husband is only barely remembered
counting out rubles into his hand.

Sunday School

A damp church basement
and organ music leaking
through the heating vent.

The minister's wife cradling
a bible worn and leathery
as a baseball mitt
in the flowery folds of her lap,

bi-focaled, reading

what exactly? All I can remember
is the baby Jesus born
into straw and sawdust,

that he was never a kid,

that he died
at 33
with a nest of thorns on his head ...

and then, when it was over upstairs, dad
dodging the collection plate,
dodging the minister's compulsory handshake,

dad in his clean Sunday suit
letting his tie flap out the window
on the car ride home.

Holocaust

My mother says
that pool is a cesspool,

whatever that means, so
I go Sundays with David's family,
with his bawling sister
and the old man, Goldfinger,

who never swims.

Poolside he swivels his
largish rump into a canvas chair,
wags at us his warning finger
fitted with its mighty ring –

*No splashes, you kids, or maybe
you want I come in –*

the biggest ring I've ever seen.

Poolside he slurps Cream Sodas
through an adjustable straw
and strokes the white hair
on his chest, now and again
slapping suntan oil across
bulge of belly and the dome
of his purple head.

Our white bodies flail and lash
the water into choppy waves,
a cannonball divides the pool,
and David's sister screams.

*I warn you kids,
or maybe you want
I come in and teach you a thing –*

Holocaust

and then bouncing David's sister
on his knee, telling her
go now be a good girl,
zayde is tired,
go run get zayde a Cream Soda,

and don't run, he says,

pointing the finger again,

and wait, he says, *come back, come back*
take also, yes,
a lemon popsicle for you.

In the water that day
I ask hey where is Goldfinger's wife,

and David says.

Dying

is as natural as breathing

Who in the hell writes these things?
I want to ask my doctor
if he knows what we're given
to read in his waiting room.
But I don't. He says
take a deep breath, and hold ...

good, he says, now breathe normally ...

and I never can, I can never get it
quite right again,
                        not until
he's pronounced me fit to live,
and even then not until
I've cleared his little white room

and walked the immaculate hall
where the hospital's ghostly benefactors
line the walls, and pressed my weight
against the big revolving door,
tumbling into the sunny afternoon,
mildly stunned that it's there.

Family Album

In one picture
snapped at the beach,
my hand, just my hand
in the top right corner.

The fingers splayed
like a child's depiction
of a radiant sun.

It could be anyone.

Trying to swim out,
trying to swim in.

Titanic

Now to imagine
the myriad fish swimming
through the metalwork –

God or no God –

home.

Forest

She said *now then*
I would like each of you

to make a tree
with your body

and we were delighted
to forget everything

we had learned all day
about staying within the lines.

Standing in our numbered rows
we stretched and stretched, embracing

the enormous air, our fingers
splayed, heels rising up

off the floor, bodies grunting, sweating,
trembling to be trees. One

poked another in the head
with a pencil. *Sharp branch*

he announced.

Nature

On rainy Sundays
we go sometimes to Russia

and I lie innocently

out in the deep dark woods
under a white tablecloth.

My son insists
I am a father

and he is a brown bear.

It goes this way.
He gets hungry

and by and by
I am chosen.

Easter

The sun's finally out
and with his stepdad a boy
builds a newspaper boat
they both half-believe
the snowmelt will float.

Things Pitched

battles

and a rationale
for the same,

curveballs,
change-ups,

a perfect game

Substitute

We were going at her pretty good
as we felt was our right
on a Friday afternoon in June,
when all of a sudden, grinding
her busy chalk into the blackboard,
snapping it cleanly in two, she wheeled
as though to face us; but her scalding eyes
fastened on a spot just above our heads,
and her voice, this once, was steady
as a metronome, saying
she deserved our respect, saying
she deserved that goddam fucking much.

Well, we stopped.
We did not move to breathe.

The moment passed. Summer gusted in
the open classroom window, billowing
the thick black curtain like a salty sail.
And one year later, when word
got around how she had died,
we knew, we had all
the answers.

Nothing

There is nothing to teach us
nothing. I watched you die
and something went out of the world,
but I don't know just what.
Bills still arrive in your name,
the watch you wore still runs.
I don't pity you,
or envy you either.
As for myself, I am still myself
and my body makes a steady sound.
I don't suppose you can hear me.

After the Silent Era

In a rented room, Chaplin,
blacklisted and alone,

and the ringing, the endless ringing
of an unplugged telephone.

Today's Decapitation

Everyone mishears the question
at first.

Like you have a foreign accent.

Like it's a payphone you're looking for,
the nearest payphone.

The question is repeated,
the hard word broken
into syllables.

Bystanders draw their children near because
you have broken a word into syllables
and must therefore be treated
like a person who will stop at nothing,

until finally, with a great rummaging through
lip gloss and keys and subway tokens,
a schedule, folded and refolded, materializes.

Elegy

Now are you taken
in hand like a zoo animal.

You are dead, and we trust
regularly fed.

The time has come to scratch
there. We who loved you

are safely lodged behind glass.
You are free at last to forget us.

Frequency

That they frequent
the mall is a fact.
But that's just one
place they turn up.
Humming in the cereal
aisle or knotting
a tie in the elevator.
They are often half-
seen squinting hard
at the No
Re-entry signs
at the ballpark.
Go lie down
under the grass
we tell the dead.
But the dead
don't listen.
Dead don't care.
They give no
more thought
to our fundamental
separateness
than music
minds walls.
And there's no radio.
No radio
and the dead
own all the stations.
They are people
we love still
and man
do they know it.

The Elephants

First the soft music of chains
sweeping the floor
and the children whispering *now
now*
and then

the two Africans
emerge, nudged along
by a small uniformed man
pushing a broom
at their feet.

Their mud-caked flanks sway
and jostle and join, raising
bright dust and stink.

More children arrive,
clamoring to touch, extending
their grateful hands

here, elephant, here.

Now look
how their supple trunks
casually collide, then hook
and swing and divide again.

Small wonder they smile
with furrowed eyes, like people
who've come to the end
of saying anything.

Angel

I was out of candy.

It said
my halo blowed off,
my wings is really for pretend,
my boots is not the kind they wear
        except when it's raining.

It said
I seen your light.

A Note About the Author

Photograph: © Chrisoula Andreou

Mike White grew up in Montreal, Canada. He received a master's degree from McGill University and a doctorate from the University of Utah. His first poetry collection, *How to Make a Bird with Two Hands* (Word Works), was awarded the 2011 Washington Prize. White's poems have appeared in journals including *The New Republic*, *Ploughshares*, *Poetry*, *The Threepenny Review*, and *The Yale Review*. His work is also featured online at *Poetry Daily* and *Verse Daily*. He lives with his family in Salt Lake City.

A Note About the Anthony Hecht Poetry Prize

The Anthony Hecht Poetry Prize was inaugurated in 2005 and is awarded on an annual basis to the best first or second collection of poems submitted.

FIRST ANNUAL HECHT PRIZE
Judge: J. D. McClatchy
Winner: Morrie Creech, *Field Knowledge*

SECOND ANNUAL HECHT PRIZE
Judge: Mary Jo Salter
Winner: Erica Dawson, *Big-Eyed Afraid*

THIRD ANNUAL HECHT PRIZE
Judge: Richard Wilbur
Winner: Rose Kelleher, *Bundle o' Tinder*

FOURTH ANNUAL HECHT PRIZE
Judge: Alan Shapiro
Winner: Carrie Jerrell, *After the Revival*

FIFTH ANNUAL HECHT PRIZE
Judge: Rosanna Warren
Winner: Matthew Ladd, *The Book of Emblems*

SIXTH ANNUAL HECHT PRIZE
Judge: James Fenton
Winner: Mark Kraushaar, *The Uncertainty Principle*

SEVENTH ANNUAL HECHT PRIZE
Judge: Mark Strand
Winner: Chris Andrews, *Lime Green Chair*

EIGHTH ANNUAL HECHT PRIZE
Judge: Charles Simic
Winner: Shelley Puhak, *Guinevere in Baltimore*

A Note About the Anthony Hecht Poetry Prize

NINTH ANNUAL HECHT PRIZE
Judge: Heather McHugh
Winner: Geoffrey Brock, *Voices Bright Flags*

TENTH ANNUAL HECHT PRIZE
Judge: Anthony Thwaite
Winner: Jaimee Hills, *How to Avoid Speaking*

ELEVENTH ANNUAL HECHT PRIZE
Judge: Eavan Boland
Winner: Austin Allen, *Pleasures of the Game*

TWELFTH ANNUAL HECHT PRIZE
Judge: Gjertrud Schnackenberg
Winner: Mike White, *Addendum to a Miracle*

For further information, please visit Waywiser's website at

waywiser-press.com

Other Books from Waywiser

POETRY
Austin Allen, *Pleasures of the Game*
Al Alvarez, *New & Selected Poems*
Chris Andrews, *Lime Green Chair*
George Bradley, *A Few of Her Secrets*
Geoffrey Brock, *Voices Bright Flags*
Robert Conquest, *Blokelore & Blokesongs*
Robert Conquest, *Penultimata*
Morri Creech, *Field Knowledge*
Morri Creech, *The Sleep of Reason*
Peter Dale, *One Another*
Erica Dawson, *Big-Eyed Afraid*
B. H. Fairchild, *The Art of the Lathe*
David Ferry, *On This Side of the River: Selected Poems*
Jeffrey Harrison, *The Names of Things: New & Selected Poems*
Joseph Harrison, *Identity Theft*
Joseph Harrison, *Shakespeare's Horse*
Joseph Harrison, *Someone Else's Name*
Joseph Harrison, ed., *The Hecht Prize Anthology, 2005-2009*
Anthony Hecht, *Collected Later Poems*
Anthony Hecht, *The Darkness and the Light*
Jaimee Hills, *How to Avoid Speaking*
Hilary S. Jacqmin, *Missing Persons*
Carrie Jerrell, *After the Revival*
Stephen Kampa, *Bachelor Pad*
Rose Kelleher, *Bundle o' Tinder*
Mark Kraushaar, *The Uncertainty Principle*
Matthew Ladd, *The Book of Emblems*
J. D. McClatchy, *Plundered Hearts: New and Selected Poems*
Dora Malech, *Shore Ordered Ocean*
Jérôme Luc Martin, *The Gardening Fires: Sonnets and Fragments*
Eric McHenry, *Odd Evening*
Eric McHenry, *Potscrubber Lullabies*
Eric McHenry and Nicholas Garland, *Mommy Daddy Evan Sage*
Timothy Murphy, *Very Far North*
Ian Parks, *Shell Island*
V. Penelope Pelizzon, *Whose Flesh is Flame, Whose Bone is Time*
Chris Preddle, *Cattle Console Him*
Shelley Puhak, *Guinevere in Baltimore*
Christopher Ricks, ed., *Joining Music with Reason:*
34 Poets, British and American, Oxford 2004-2009
Daniel Rifenburgh, *Advent*
Mary Jo Salter, *It's Hard to Say: Selected Poems*
W. D. Snodgrass, *Not for Specialists: New & Selected Poems*

Other Books from Waywiser

Mark Strand, *Almost Invisible*
Mark Strand, *Blizzard of One*
Bradford Gray Telford, *Perfect Hurt*
Matthew Thorburn, *This Time Tomorrow*
Cody Walker, *Shuffle and Breakdown*
Cody Walker, *The Self-Styled No-Child*
Cody Walker, *The Trumpiad*
Deborah Warren, *The Size of Happiness*
Clive Watkins, *Already the Flames*
Clive Watkins, *Jigsaw*
Richard Wilbur, *Anterooms*
Richard Wilbur, *Mayflies*
Richard Wilbur, *Collected Poems 1943-2004*
Norman Williams, *One Unblinking Eye*
Greg Williamson, *A Most Marvelous Piece of Luck*
Greg Williamson, *The Hole Story of Kirby the Sneak and Arlo the True*
Stephen Yenser, *Stone Fruit*

Fiction
Gregory Heath, *The Entire Animal*
Mary Elizabeth Pope, *Divining Venus*
K. M. Ross, *The Blinding Walk*
Gabriel Roth, *The Unknowns**
Matthew Yorke, *Chancing It*

Illustrated
Nicholas Garland, *I wish ...*
Eric McHenry and Nicholas Garland, *Mommy Daddy Evan Sage*
Greg Williamson, *The Hole Story of Kirby the Sneak and Arlo the True*

Non-Fiction
Neil Berry, *Articles of Faith: The Story of British Intellectual Journalism*
Mark Ford, *A Driftwood Altar: Essays and Reviews*
Richard Wollheim, *Germs: A Memoir of Childhood*

* Co-published with Picador